Sunshine

Pupil's Book 4

Englisch ab Klasse 1

Erarbeitet von
Tanja Beattie (Ebersberg)
Stefanie Keller (Konstanz)
Nadine Kerler (Ulm)
Daniela Röbers (Erkelenz)
Caroline Schröder (München)
Maria Skejic (Frankfurt am Main)
Gertrud Steinhausen (Ratingen)

Auf der Grundlage der Ausgabe von
Birgit Hollbrügge
und Ulrike Kraaz

Cornelsen

In deinem Buch findest du gelbe Notizzettel mit Symbolen:

Hier erfährst du mehr über die englische Sprache.

Hier erfährst du mehr über Großbritannien.

Hier sollst du mehr zu einem Thema herausfinden.

Manche Aufgaben bearbeitest du zuerst alleine und dann gemeinsam:

Think-Pair-Share

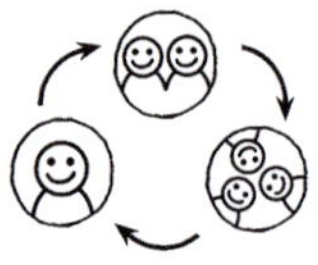

Think: Überlege, wie du die Aufgabe lösen könntest.

Pair: Tausche dich mit einem Partner aus.

Share: Überprüfe die Ergebnisse mit der Gruppe/Klasse.

Symbols

draw or write

talk

read

listen to your partner or teacher

extra

listen to the CD

explain the rules/task in German

Contents

Note

***Wh**ere?* = Wo?
*you **w**ere* = du warst

1 Talk about the picture.

I can see …

2 Read the speech bubbles with a partner.

3 Talk about holidays. Ask a partner:
Where were you in your holidays?
Say: *In my holidays I was …*

I was
in the USA.
Where were
you?

☆ Do a class survey.

OK.
How were your holidays, Emily?
Were you in Rome, Kate?
Yes. It was great!
I was at home.
Where were you in your holidays, Harry?
Where was Samir?
He was in Germany.
Are these your pictures?
Yes, they are.
Berlin
Rome
Wales
Scotland
Alps
Germany
Spain
Roma

☆ What's in the classroom? Think. Pair. Share.
There is … / There are …

1 Talk about the pictures.

In picture one I can see …

There is … / There are …

2 Listen. Point to the pictures.

3 Read. Talk to a partner. Say: *What do you do in the … ? – In the …*

What do you eat for breakfast? Say: *I eat …*

In the morning

I get up.
I have breakfast.
I go to school.

In the afternoon

I do my homework.
I meet my friends.

In the evening

I have dinner.
I go to bed.

Good morning!
1
Pass me the butter, please.
2
Bye!
3
I love English. It's my favourite subject!
4
Hi!
5
Oh, I hate carrot soup!
6
Good night!
7

4 Talk about Emily's timetable. Say: *On Monday, Emily has Maths, …*

5 Listen. What day is it?

Time	Monday	Tuesday	Wednesday	Thursday	Friday
9.00-9.30	ASSEMBLY				
9.30-10.30	Maths	Maths	English	Music	Maths
10.30-10.45	PLAY				
10.45-11.45	English	German	Maths	Maths	English
11.45-12.30	LUNCH				
12.30-1.15	QUIET				
1.15-2.15	Music	Computers	Science	English	Art
2.15-3.15	German	P.E.	P.E.	Art	Computers

Note

In Großbritannien beginnt der Schultag mit einer großen Versammlung. Diese nennt man *assembly*.

After lunch I have …

Write your own timetable.

1 A trip to London

1 Talk about the map.

I can see …

There is … /
There are …

2 Read the texts. Find the sights on the map.
Say: *Number one is …*

3 Listen to your teacher.
Find the sights on the map.

(1) **Tower Bridge** is a very famous bridge. It can open to let big ships through. It takes about 90 seconds to open.

(2) **London Zoo** is one of the oldest zoos in the world. You can see about 750 different kinds of animals there.

(3) **Buckingham Palace** is the Queen's London home. On top of Buckingham Palace you can see the Union flag.

(4) **Big Ben** is the name of a bell. The bell is inside the clock tower of Westminster Palace.

Note

The London underground is called the 'Tube'.

4 Look at the map. Listen and find the way.

☆ Say where and when they go. How do they get there?
Say: *They take the … / They go by …*

☆ Choose one sight. Make a poster.

Think. Pair. Share.

Note

Find out more about the sights 7 (Tower of London) and 8 (Trafalgar Square).

6
UNDERGROUND
7
4
5
1
UNDERGROUND

(5) The **London Eye** is the biggest observation wheel in the world. It is 135 metres high.

(6) **Madame Tussauds** is a famous wax museum. You can see film stars, sports stars, pop stars and the Royal Family there. Who is your favourite star?

Let's talk

5 Read the dialogue. Talk to a partner.

☆ More: Make up your own dialogue.

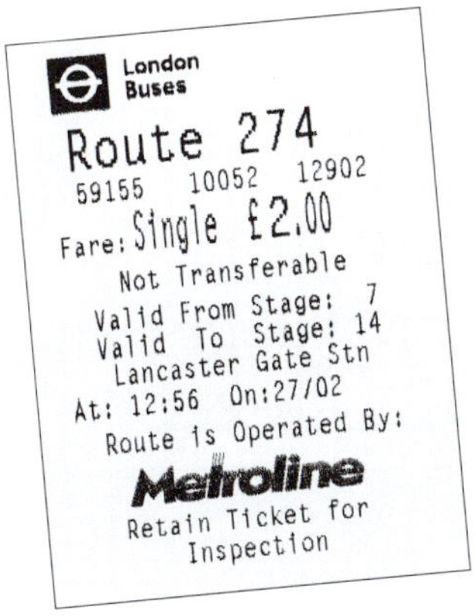

London Buses
Route 274
59155 10052 12902
Fare: Single £2.00
Not Transferable
Valid From Stage: 7
Valid To Stage: 14
Lancaster Gate Stn
At: 12:56 On:27/02
Route is Operated By:
Metroline
Retain Ticket for Inspection

A ticket to Big Ben, please.
That's £2, please.

1 Look at the pictures. Talk about the pictures.

2 Read the postcards. Say the numbers.

3 Listen to your partner. Point to the right postcard.

★ When was Harry's birthday?
What's the name of Harry's grandma?
Who was on top of the London Eye?

Note

Look at Kate's SMS.
What does she write?

1

2

3

LONDON EYE

Hello Jack,

I'm in London with Kate and her dad.
It's super! Thursday was my birthday.
We went on a boat trip on the River
Thames to the London Eye. It was
great. I could see Buckingham Palace
from the top of the London Eye.

Harry

Dear Mum,

I like London. It's great!
Yesterday it was Harry's birthday.
Today we went to Hyde Park to eat
some ice cream and to play football.
We walked over Tower Bridge, too.
What a big bridge! You must go and
see Tower Bridge. It opens in the
middle. See you on Saturday.

Love, Kate

Mrs William
12 Morgan Stree

Dear Grandma,

How are you? I'm in London with my
friend Kate and her dad.
It's Tuesday. London is great.
I like sitting at the top of the
red buses. Here's a picture of
Big Ben. Big Ben is a bell inside the
clock tower!

I hope you come to my
birthday party on Sunday.

Love, Harry

2nd

Mrs Benson
5 Birch Street
Portsmouth
Hants PO12 2TB

12:38
Hi Mum, Lndn is
gr8! 2day we are
going to Tower
Bridge. CU next
Mon.
Kate X

1 Read the dialogues.

2 Act out the dialogues.

Hi, can I help you? What would you like to drink?
I'd like some water, please.
I'd like some tea, please.
1

What about you? What would you like to eat?
I'd like a cheese and ham sandwich and a salad, please.
Here you are. Anything else?
I'd like a chicken sandwich, please. Do you have chips?
Sorry, we don't have chips.
2

Here you are.
Thank you.
Thank you. Can we have the bill, please?
3

How much is it?
That's £8, please.
Here you are.
Thank you. Bye.
4

Write a (shopping) list. Think. Pair. Share.

bread · cheese · chicken · chips · chocolate · ham · sweets · tea · tomatoes · water · ...

Note

chips = Pommes (frites)

3 What do you eat/drink for lunch?
Say: *I eat .../I drink ...*

1 Listen to the story.

2 Read the story.

3 Act it out.

Note

Who was the Earl of Sandwich?
Find out more!

Note

In which other countries are there still kings or queens? Find out!

22 **1** Listen. Point to the pictures.

2 Read the sentences.

People in Britain love the Royal Family.

Royal guards in front of Buckingham Palace.

The Royals are everywhere.

3 Read the sentences. Find the right pictures.

Talk about activities and times. Say: *At 10 a.m., William …*

One day in the life of two Royals.

Note

a.m. = in the morning
p.m. = in the afternoon

08:00 a.m.	Kate takes her dog for a walk.
10:00 a.m.	William visits a football team.
12:00	Kate and William have lunch.
02:00 p.m.	Kate visits pupils at a London school.
07:30 p.m.	Kate and William are at a concert.

2 All year round

Note

cloud – cloud**y**
sun – sunn**y**
wind – …

Find out more!

1 Read the sentences. Talk about the pictures.
Say: *I can see … / There is / are …*

1

It's very cold and snowy today. Look at my snowman!

2

It's foggy in London.

3

What a windy day!

4

It's sunny and hot. I love eating ice cream!

5

What a cold and rainy day!

6

It's cold and cloudy today.

2 What do you wear when it's hot / cold? What can you do?
Make a poster. Think. Pair. Share.

clothes

boots · cap · coat · dress · hat · jacket · jeans · pullover · sandals · scarf · shirt · shoes · skirt · T-shirt

sports and hobbies

play football / tennis · read a book · ride a horse · ride a bike · sing · ski · snowboard · swim · …

It's sunny and hot today! I'm looking for my sunglasses.

Let's talk

1 Read the dialogue. Talk to a partner.
☆ More: Make up your own dialogue.

Hi, how are you?
I'm OK.
What's the weather like in London?
It's great, 20 degrees and sunny.

2 Look at the pictures. Talk to a partner. Say: *In Rome it's …*

1
Rome (15°C)

2
New York (-3°C)

3
SUNDAY
MANCHESTER
32°C
Feels like: 32°C
Humidity: 63%
Pressure: 1012.1 MB
Wind: 23 KM/H
Sunrise: 5:52 AM
Sunset: 8:12 PM
MONDAY 29°C
TUESDAY 25°C
WEDNESDAY 23°C
THURSDAY 26°C

4
Paris (25°C)

5
Ankara (33°C)

6
London (13°C)

In Manchester it's sunny.

> **Note**
>
> How to say the day and date:
>
> Today it is Monday.
> It's the fourth of September 2018.

1 Read and match.

Hi, I'm Robin. My birthday is in September, in autumn. In autumn, the leaves turn red and yellow. When it is windy, I like flying my kite. Do you like my birthday cake?

Hello, my name is Oona. I was born in summer, in July. When it is sunny and hot, I like eating ice cream. What do you do in summer?

Hi, I'm Arian. My birthday is in April, in spring. In spring, there are lots of flowers. I like looking for Easter eggs. Do you like my tree?

Hello, my name is Mathilda. My birthday is in winter, in February. Sometimes it is cold and snowy on my birthday. I like playing in the snow. Do you like my snowman?

2 Answer the questions.

- When is Robin's/Arian's/… birthday? Say: *Robin's birthday is in …*
- What's the weather like in spring/summer/…? Say: *In spring, it's …*
- What do the children like? Say: *Robin likes …*

★ When is your birthday? Say the season and the date: *It's in … on the …*

★ What day is it today? What's the date? Say: *Today it is … It's the …*

1 Talk about the pictures.
When is the wind helpful? When is the wind dangerous?

1

2

3

4

5

6

2 Read the rhyme.
Say the rhyme.

The kites go up, the kites go down.
See how they fly all over the town.
The children run and jump and play,
Because they love a windy day.

3 Do the experiment with your teacher.

You need:

a glass bottle | a candle | matches

4 Explain.

1. Put the candle behind the bottle.
2. Blow hard on the bottle. What happens to the candle?

Watch the film.

What I can do and say

A word web

food and shopping

bread
butter
cheese
chicken
egg
ham
salad
tea
tomato
water

Hi, can I help you?
Can I have a/an/some ..., please?
I'd like ...
How much is it?
It's ...
Here you are.
Thank you.

apple · chocolate
fruit · sweets

I eat/drink ... · How many ...?

Make your own word web

Think. Pair. Share.

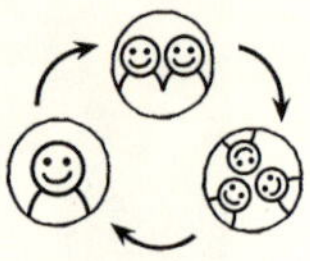

time

school

birthdays

When is (your birthday)?–It's on the 4th of May 2018. · My birthday is in May./It's in spring. · Happy Birthday! · What day is it today?–Today it is ... · What's the date?–It's the 4th of May. · I like/I don't like ... · I have English at 9:30. · My favourite subject is English/... · My teacher is ... · Excuse me, please. What time is it?–It's ... · I don't know.

What can you do or say in English? Think!

I can ...
- ... say the words.
- ... write the words.
- ... ask and answer questions.

What do you want to be better at?

What I can do and say

How to talk about pictures:

You don't know the word in English?

Ask your teacher or partner.

Mime!

Play 'Mime and guess'.

3 At the museum

1 Which animals are in the museum?

There is … / There are …

2 Read the speech bubbles. Talk to a partner.

I want to see the crocodiles.
Which animals do you want to see?
I want to see the whales. What about you?

29
crocodiles
18
dinosaurs

★ Can you find the museum on the London map? (Look at page 6/7.)

This is the Natural History Museum in London.

Look, there's a mole in the museum.

upstairs
downstairs

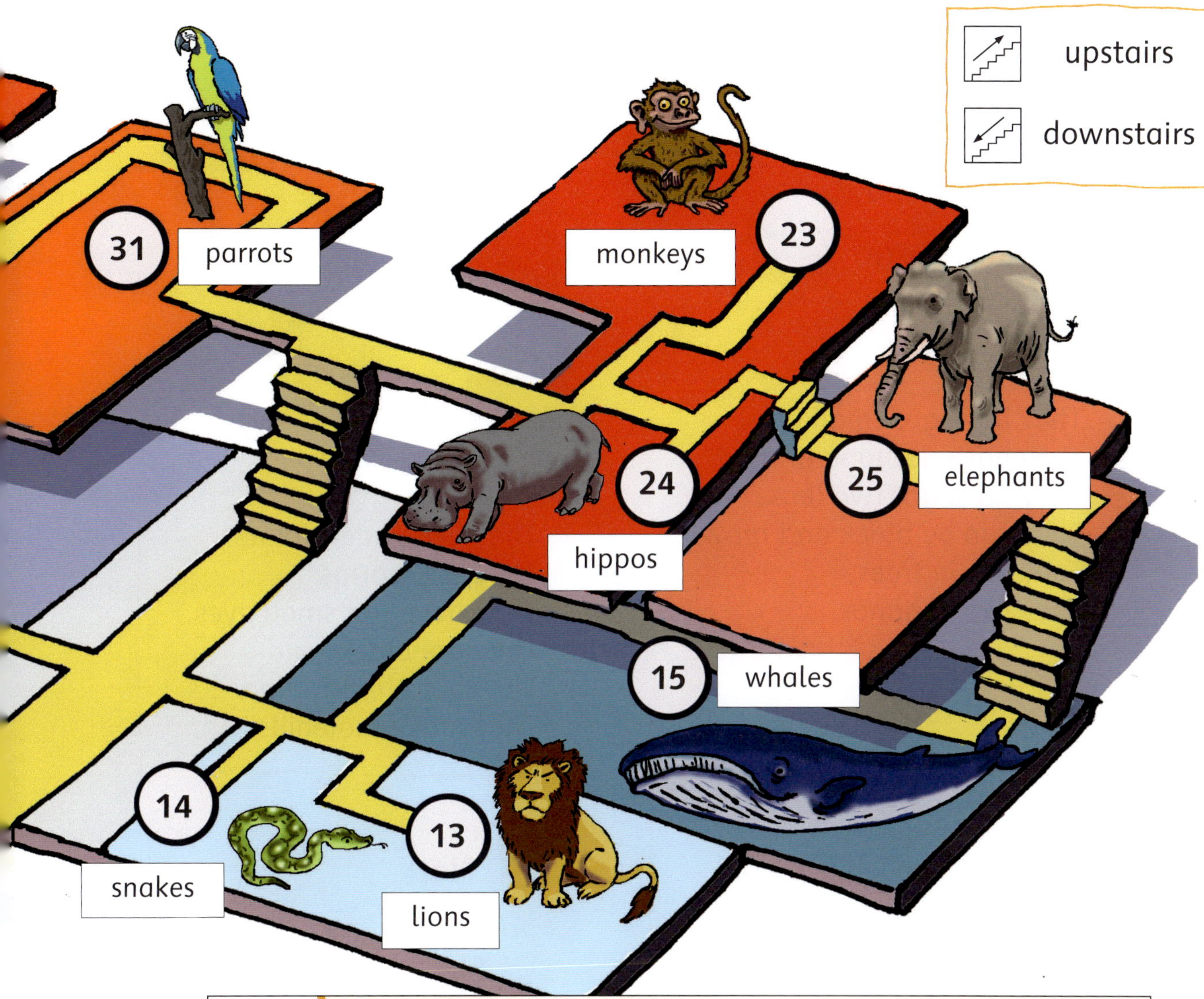
31 parrots
monkeys 23
24 hippos
25 elephants
15 whales
14 snakes
13 lions

Let's talk

3 Read the dialogue. Talk to a partner.

☆ More: Make up your own dialogue.

Excuse me, please. Where are the whales?
They are downstairs, in room 15.
You go straight ahead, then you turn left.
WC

1 Read the texts. Which animal is it?

Think of one more animal.
Talk, draw or show.

Think. Pair. Share.

They have got small ears.
They have got long arms.
They have got two legs.
They can be black and brown.
They live in trees.
They like bananas.

They live underground.
They eat worms.
They have got small eyes.
They are black.
They are almost blind.
They make molehills.

It lives in the jungle.
It is grey.
It has got big ears.
It has got two white teeth.
It has got small eyes.
It has got big legs.
It eats leaves and grass.

Note

no – know
Say:
***Know** your text.*
*They have **no** feet.*

2 Read the presentation rules.

I want to talk about crocodiles. The crocodile is a wild animal …
Nile Crocodile

- Make notes.
- Know your text.
- Speak loudly.
- Look at the class.
- Show pictures.

1 Talk about the pictures.

2 Read the story.

☆ Complete the speech bubbles. Work with a partner.

There is … / There are …

I can see …

It's 6 o'clock. The museum isn't open.
Closed
Upstairs on the left. There's the lion.
I wish I had a lion's strong teeth.
Downstairs and right. There's the elephant.
I wish I had an elephant's big ears.
…
…
Oh no! Help!
It was just a dream.

More to explore: **The Jurassic Coast**

Jurassic Coast
London

36 **1** Listen. Point to the pictures.

2 Read the texts. Find the matching pictures.

☆ Find out more about dinosaurs. Think. Pair. Share.

1 
Jurassic Coast

2 
dinosaur fossil

3 
dinosaur footprint

4 
ammonites

5 
a fish

6 
dinosaur museum

The Jurassic Coast is a region in South England.

At the Jurassic Coast you can often find ammonites.

A dinosaur walked here a long time ago. Look at its footprint!

At the dinosaur museum in Dorchester you can learn a lot about dinosaurs.

Look, that was a fish! It lived a long time ago.

This is the fossil of a dinosaur.

Watch the film.

→ DVD 3

Note

Viele englische Kinder besuchen während oder nach der Schule einen Klub. Gibt es so etwas auch an deiner Schule?

1 Read the posters with a partner. Listen and name the club.

2 Work with a partner. Talk about the clubs. Look at the speech bubbles.

37

3 Listen. What club do the children want to go to?

Make your own club poster. Use a dictionary.

Think. Pair. Share.

Where's the dance club?

It's in ...

When's the ... club?

It's on ...

Girls' football club
Girls can play football!
When: Wednesday
Where: In the park
Dance to your favourite songs at the
Dance club
When: Thursday
Where: Room 12
Dog? Cat? Guinea pig?
What is your favourite animal?
Pet club
When: Tuesday
Where: Room 6a
Do you like computers?
Then come to the
Computer club
When: Wednesday
Where: Computer room
Do you like computers?
Judo club
Do judo with your friends.
When: Monday
Where: Room 4
Move your body at the
Fit kids club
When: Friday
Where: High Street fitness club

1 Listen. What can Linda do?

2 Read the dialogue with a partner.

Make up your own dialogue.

Think. Pair. Share.

Note

I cannot = I can't

Hi, **Linda**. Can I ask you some questions about sport?
Yes, OK.
What's your favourite sport?
My favourite sport is **skiing**.
What about tennis? Can you **play tennis**?
No, I cannot play tennis. But I can **play table tennis**.
Do you go to the **table tennis club on Tuesday**?
No, I go to the computer club **on Tuesday**.
Thanks for the interview. Bye!
You're welcome. Bye!

Story: **Giraffes can't dance**

43 **1** Listen. Point to the pictures.

2 Read the story.

Gerald the giraffe likes dancing. But when he dances, his legs get in the way and he falls down.

The other animals laugh at Gerald when he dances. They shout out: 'Giraffes can't dance!' Poor Gerald! He leaves the dance floor. He feels sad and lonely.

A cricket sees Gerald and says: 'Don't be sad. You can dance! Everyone can dance. Just listen to the music around you!'

Gerald listens to the music. His legs start to move and then his neck starts to sway. Gerald is so excited. 'I can dance. I can dance.' He feels wonderful.

The other animals see Gerald dancing. They start to clap. 'Wow, Gerald, you are a really good dancer!' they say. Gerald is so proud that he can dance. 'Thank you, thank you!' he says. Now all the animals are his friends. He feels very happy.

3 How does Gerald feel? Find the key words.

45 **1** Listen and point to the pictures.

1

2

3

4

Note

Viele englische Kinder spielen *Rounders* auf dem Schulhof. Kennst du ein ähnliches Spiel?

2 Look at the pictures. Read the rules. Talk to a partner about the rules.

3 Explain.

You need:

 a bat	 a ball	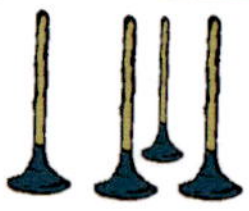 4 posts	 6-15 players

(1) Form two teams.

batting team

fielding team

(2) Choose a bowler.

bowler

(3) The bowler bowls the ball. The batter hits the ball.

(4) The batter runs from post to post.

The team with the most rounders wins.

P.E.

Watch the film.

Fächerübergreifendes Lernen: „Sports", s. HRU, S. 301-304 → DVD 4

Emails from the USA

1 Talk about the picture.

There is …/
There are …

I can see …

2 What are the friends doing?

Kate, Great Britain
Leon, Germany
Matt, USA

3 Read the questions and the answers.

4 Think of more questions. Write.

Think. Pair. Share.

Note

Sprich immer zuerst mit deiner Lehrerin, deinem Lehrer oder deinen Eltern, bevor du im Internet von dir erzählst. Dein Name, deine Adresse, deine Telefonnummer oder dein Geburtsdatum gehen nicht jeden etwas an.

STOP

What's your password?	•••••••••••
What's your name?	*My name is Kate.*
How old are you?	*I'm 10 years old.*
When's your birthday?	*It's in May.*
Where are you from?	*I'm from Great Britain.*
What's your nickname?	*Kitty*
What are your hobbies?	*dancing, swimming*

My password is top secret!

Note

Americans pay with dollars ($) and cents. How much is 1 € in $?

1 Talk about the pictures.

1

Statue of Liberty

2

Empire State Building

3

Central Park

4

Brooklyn Bridge

5

yellow cab

47 **2** Listen to Matt's rap. Point to the pictures.

3 Read the text.

Do the rap.

Welcome to New York,
Welcome to the sights,
Welcome to the city
That never sleeps at nights.

Go to Central Park,
Have a picnic in the sun.
Skate, skate, play or walk,
Have lots of fun.

New York City is the place 2 B. Yo!
New York City is the place 4 me.

The Empire State Building
Is very high.
One hundred an' three
floors up to the sky.

Over Brooklyn Bridge
You can bike, walk or ride
Or take a yellow cab
From side to side.

One more sight
You have to see
And that's the famous
Statue of Liberty.

1 Read Kate's email. What does she write about?

To: mattman@world.e-pals.com
Subject: About my family

Dear Matt,
Today I want to write about my family. I live with my mum and dad. Where do you live? Do you have a big family? My dad has got a second-hand shop. My mum is a hairdresser. I've got a sister. She's older than me. She's a shop assistant. I haven't got a brother, but I've got a lot of friends. My best friends are Harry, Samir and Emily. We like playing in Harry's garden and in the street. What do you like?

From,
Kate

2 Listen to Matt's email.

51

3 Read the text.

To: kitty@world.e-pals.com
Subject: About me

Hi Kate,
Thanks for your email. I'm ten years old. My birthday is in November. I've got a brother. He's a mechanic. And I've got a little sister. My mother is a teacher. My father is a taxi driver. I've got a small room. I've got two hamsters. I like playing with my hamsters. My hobbies are playing tennis and reading. What are your hobbies?

From,
Matt

4 Read Ben's email.

Write an answer. Think. Pair. Share.

To: epal@world.e-pals.com
Subject: finding an e-pal

Hello e-pal,
My name is Ben. I'm from England. I live in London.
I'm ten years old and I'm in class four. I like English and sports.
And I like Germany. My hobby is playing football.
What's your hobby? Please write back!

From,
Ben

Note

What's your mum's or dad's job? Look in a dictionary.

1 Talk about the pictures.

2 Read the story.

What's your dream job? Say: *I wish I was …*

→ DVD 5

1 Read the texts about John, the police officer.

2 Listen to your partner. Point to the right picture.

1

NYPD
POLICE

2

NYPD

3

Hello, my name is John.
I'm a police officer
in New York City.

In the city
we patrol by car.

You can go
very fast on a motorbike.

In Central Park
we use horses.

I can see more
from a helicopter.

Do you like my badge?

4

POLICE
DEPARTMENT
CITY OF NEW YORK

5

6

55

3 Listen. Talk to a partner.

More: Make up your own dialogue.

Do you want police, fire or ambulance?
Ambulance. My brother needs help.
What's your name?
My name is Mark.
What's your address?
32 Green Street.
Where are you?
I'm at the Empire State Building.
OK. Stay where you are.
OK.

What I can do and say

A word web

play football
ride a bike/horse
skateboard
ski
snowboard
swim
play tennis

sports and hobbies

What's your hobby?
My hobby is ...
Do you like ...?
I like .../
I don't like ...

dance · do judo/ballet · play table tennis

Have you got a ...?
Yes, I have. It's ...

Make your own word web

feelings

Think. Pair. Share.

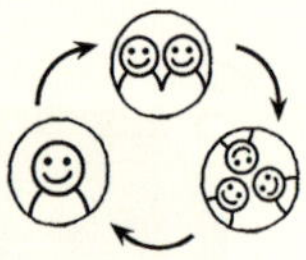

family

This is my ... · Have you got ...?–Yes, I've got .../No, I haven't got ... · He/She has got ... · How many ... have you got? · What's his/her name?–His/Her name is ... · How old is he/she?–He/She is ... · How are you?–I'm happy/sad/OK. · I'm cold/hot. · How do you feel?–I feel ... · This is my... · What are your hobbies?–My hobbies are ...

What can you do or say in English? Think!

I can ...
... say the words.
... write the words.
... ask and answer questions.

What do you want to be better at?

What I can do and say

How to present:

Think. Make notes.
Know your text.

Look at your notes.
Show pictures.
Speak slowly and loudly.
Look at the class.

Team game: 'Whispering chain'.

You need:
One set of picture cards.

cheese

1. Listen to your teacher.

che...

2. Whisper the word to the next pupil in line.

Yes, that's right.

3. Find the matching card.
Show it to your teacher.
Is it the right card?
Well done!
One point for you.

Story: **The school inspector** A school play

It's
Show time!

1 Listen.
Point to the pictures.

2 Read the story.

1
Good morning, Mrs Brown.
Sorry, I'm late.
Yes, you are, Simon. Sit down.
2
Have you got your pencils?
Yes, we have.
Give it back, Jack!
3
What a bad class you are.
That isn't right! They're good pupils.
4
Do you know about animals?
crocodile
Crocodiles are wild animals.
Of course, we do.
5
That isn't right. They're good pupils.
That was bad.

Note

Hast du schon mal eine richtige Schulinspektion erlebt? Vergleiche!

1 What did you learn?
What can you say in English?
Read the texts.

2 What's your favourite unit?
Say: *My favourite unit is unit … because …*

I know the colours and numbers in English.

I can talk about my family and friends.

I can say which pets I like.

I can talk about my school things.

I can talk about clothes.

class 3

I can talk about rooms and furniture.

I can buy food and drinks.

I can read a story book.

How did

That was OK.

That was not so good.

That was great!

I was good at …

class 4

I can say what time it is.

I can talk about the weather, seasons and my birthday month.

ou like it?

I like … because …

I don't like … because …

My favourite words are …

I want to learn more about …

I can do a presentation about animals.

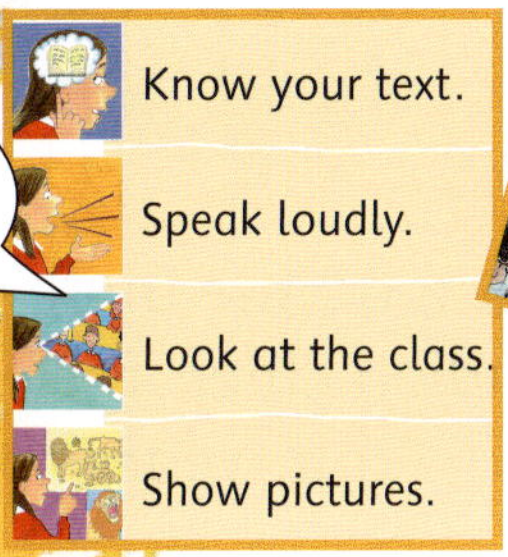
Know your text.
Speak loudly.
Look at the class.
Show pictures.

Crocodiles are wild animals …

I can say what my hobbies are.

I can read the story about Gerald the giraffe.

GIRAFFES CAN'T DANCE

I can write about myself and my family.

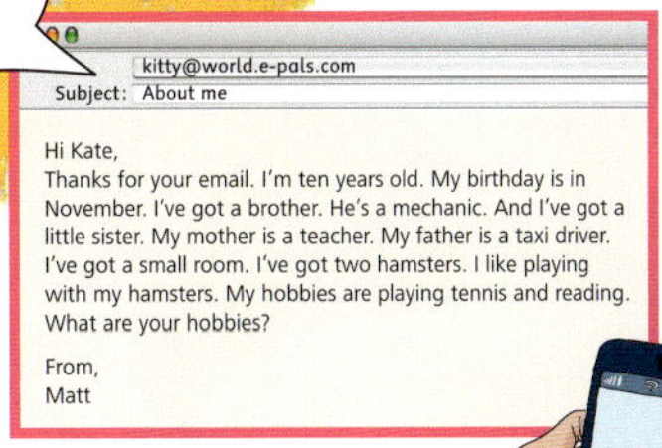
kitty@world.e-pals.com
Subject: About me

Hi Kate,
Thanks for your email. I'm ten years old. My birthday is in November. I've got a brother. He's a mechanic. And I've got a little sister. My mother is a teacher. My father is a taxi driver. I've got a small room. I've got two hamsters. I like playing with my hamsters. My hobbies are playing tennis and reading. What are your hobbies?

From,
Matt

I know about Halloween.

1 Look at the pictures. Talk.

76 2 Listen. Point to the pictures.

3 Read the story.

1

Once upon a time there was a Plains Indian chief. The Plains Indians did not wear shoes.

2
Ouch! Aaggh! Oh no! My poor feet!

There were big stones in the water.

3
This is the answer to the problem.

The medicine man had an idea: 'Let's make a carpet for the chief!'

4
Ouch! Aaggh! Oh no! My poor feet!

But it was not the answer to the problem.

5

The medicine man had a dream.

6
Thank you! The moccasins are wonderful!
You're welcome!

The medicine man had an idea. And he made the first moccasins. It was a very good idea.

1 Talk about the picture.

How many ghosts, monsters, pumpkins, skeletons, … can you see?

70 2 Listen to the rhyme.

3 Read the rhyme.

Trick or treat,
Listen to the beat.
We want only
Sweets to eat.

Trick or treat,
Smell my feet.
Give me something
Good to eat!

1 Talk about the pictures.

2 Listen to the rhyme.

3 Read the rhyme.

Say the rhyme.

Remember, remember
The fifth of November,
Gunpowder, treason and plot.
I see no reason
Why gunpowder treason
Should ever be forgot.

I wish you a
Merry Christmas
and a Happy
New Year!

73 **1** Listen to the story. Point to the pictures.

2 Read the story.

Sing the song. Find the matching pictures in the story.

Rudolph is a reindeer. He has a red and shiny nose.

The other reindeer laugh at Rudolph's nose.

Poor Rudolph is sad and lonely.

It's Christmas Eve. It's very foggy. Santa asks Rudolph for help.

Rudolph helps Santa. He guides the sleigh. He shows the reindeer the way.

Rudolph is very proud and very happy. The reindeer are his friends. They all love him. Rudolph is never sad and lonely again.

Looking at English

So verändern sich die Wörter in der Mehrzahl:
Wenn du von mehreren Dingen sprichst, hängst du ein ‚s' an.

one book – two book**s**
one apple – two apple**s**

➜ Es gibt Ausnahmen, die du dir merken musst:

one child – two child**ren**
one hobb**y** – two hobb**ies**

So sagst du, dass jemanden etwas gehört:

This is Tim**'s** book.

This is Anne**'s** pencil case.

Note

Finde Beispiele in deinem Pupil's Book!

Diese Wörter brauchst du, um Fragen zu stellen:

What? = Was?
What is this?

When? = Wann?
When is your birthday?

Where? = Wo?
Where is my book?

Who? = Wer?
Who is on the telephone?

How? = Wie?
How are you?

How many? = Wie viele?
How many children like chocolate?

How much? = Wie viel?
How much is the orange juice?

➜ Es gibt Ausnahmen, die du dir merken musst:

What time is it? = Wie spät ist es?
What's your name? = Wie heißt du?

So fangen viele Fragen an:

Do you like …? = Magst du …?
Can I have …? = Kann ich … haben?
Have you got …? = Hast du …?
Are you happy/sad/angry? = Bist du glücklich/traurig/wütend?

Looking at English

So kannst du über dich und andere sprechen:

I am

you are

he is

she is

it is

we are

you are

they are

Manche Wörter werden abgekürzt: I am = I'm

I am = I'm
you are = you're
he is = he's
she is = she's
it is = it's
we are = we're
you are = you're
they are = they're

I cannot = I can't
where is = where's
what is = what's
I would like = I'd like
I have got = I've got

Note

Finde Beispiele in deinem Pupil's Book!

Manche Wörter haben mehrere Bedeutungen:

you	=	du, ihr
it	=	er, sie, es
the	=	der, die, das

Word list

A
about über
afternoon Nachmittag
again noch einmal, wieder
angry verärgert
animal Tier
answer antworten, Antwort
Art Kunst (Schulfach)
ask fragen
at bei, im, um
aunt Tante
autumn Herbst

B
back Rücken
bad schlecht
ballet Ballett
basketball Basketball
be sein
because weil
behind hinter
belly Bauch
bend beugen
big groß
birthday Geburtstag
blackboard Tafel
blow out auspusten
boat Boot
bonfire Lagerfeuer
book Buch
boy Junge
bread Brot
breakfast Frühstück
brother Bruder
bus Bus
bus driver Busfahrer/in
bush Busch
but aber
butter Butter
buy kaufen

C
calendar Kalender
camel Kamel
can können
candle Kerze
car Auto
caretaker Hausmeister
carpet Teppich
cent (hier: amerikanischer) Cent
chair Stuhl
cheese Käse
chicken Huhn
chips Pommes frites
chocolate Schokolade
Christmas Weihnachten
city Großstadt
clap klatschen
class Klasse
classroom Klassenraum
clock Uhr
clock tower Glockenturm
cloudy wolkig
club AG, Klub, Verein
colour (in) Farbe, ausmalen
come kommen
Computers (I.C.T.) Computer (Schulfach)
crocodile Krokodil
cut out ausschneiden

D
daffodil Osterglocke
dance tanzen
dangerous gefährlich
date Datum
day Tag
Dear ... Liebe/r ...
degree(s) Grad
dinosaur Dinosaurier
dinner Abendessen
do machen, tun
do ballet Ballett tanzen
do judo Judo betreiben
dollar ($) (hier: amerikanischer) Dollar
door Tür
downstairs unten
draw zeichnen
dream Traum
drink trinken, Getränk
driver Fahrer

E
ear Ohr
eat essen
egg Ei
elephant Elefant
email E-Mail
England England
English englisch, Englisch (Schulfach)
e-pal E-Mail-Freund/in
euro (€) Euro
evening Abend
eye Auge

Word list

Englisch–Deutsch

F

famous berühmt
father Vater
Father Christmas Weihnachtsmann
favourite Lieblings-
feed füttern
fireworks Feuerwerk
flag Flagge
flap auf und ab bewegen
fly fliegen
foggy neblig
food Essen
foot, feet Fuß, Füße
football Fußball
forget vergessen
forward vorwärts
Friday Freitag
from aus, von

G

game Spiel
German deutsch, Deutsch (Schulfach)
Germany Deutschland
ghost Geist
giraffe Giraffe
girl Mädchen
give geben
glue kleben
go gehen
Good luck! Viel Glück!
Goodness gracious! Du meine Güte!
grandfather, grandpa Großvater, Opa
grandmother, grandma Großmutter, Oma
Great Britain Großbritannien
gunpowder Schießpulver

H

hairdresser Friseur/in
half past halb (Uhrzeit)
Halloween Halloween
ham Schinken
happen geschehen
happy glücklich
hate hassen
have (got) haben
have to müssen
he er
head Kopf
hello hallo
help helfen, Hilfe
helpful hilfreich
her ihr/ihre
here hier
hippo Nilpferd
his sein/seine
hobby Hobby
holidays Ferien
(at) home zu Hause
hop hopsen, springen
hope hoffen
horse Pferd
hot heiß, warm
house Haus
how wie
how many wie viele
how much wie viel

I

idea Idee
ill krank
in in
in front of vor
inspector Inspektor/in, Schulrat/-rätin
is ist
it es

J

job Beruf, Job
judo Judo
jump springen
jungle Dschungel

K

king König
kite Drachen
knee Knie
know kennen, wissen

L

late spät
leaf, leaves Blatt, Blätter
left links
leg Bein
lesson Schulstunde
Let's go! Los!
lettuce Kopfsalat
line Linie, Reihe
lion Löwe
listening to music Musik hören
little klein
live leben, wohnen
long lang

look at betrachten
loud, loudly laut
love lieben
Love, ... Liebe Grüße ...
lunch Mittagessen

M

make machen
many viel/e
matches Streichhölzer
Maths Mathe (Schulfach)
mechanic Mechaniker/in
meeting friends Freunde treffen
miss a turn aussetzen
Monday Montag
monkey Affe
morning Morgen
mother Mutter
motorbike Motorrad
move (sich) bewegen
much viel
museum Museum
Music Musik (Schulfach)
my mein/e

N

name Name
next to neben
nice nett
nickname Spitzname
nose Nase
not nicht
notes Noten, Notizen
number Nummer

O

o'clock ... Uhr
of course natürlich
old alt
on auf
open offen, öffnen

P

P.E. (= Physical Education) Sport (Schulfach)
paper Papier
parrot Papagei
password Passwort
photo Foto
picture Bild
plane Flugzeug
play spielen, Theaterspiel
please bitte
plot Verschwörung
point to auf ... zeigen
police officer Polizist/in
police station Polizeiwache
postcard Postkarte
present Geschenk
pumpkin Kürbis
pupil Schüler/in
purple lila
put legen, stellen

Q

quarter past/to viertel nach/vor (Uhrzeit)
queen Königin
quiet leise

R

rainy regnerisch
read lesen
remember erinnern
rhyme Reim
ride a horse reiten
right rechts
river Fluss
rose Rose
run laufen

S

sad traurig
salad (zubereiteter) Salat
Santa, Santa Claus Weihnachtsmann (in den USA)
Saturday Samstag
savannah Savanne
say sagen
scared verängstigt
Science Sachunterricht (Schulfach)
sea Meer
season Jahreszeit
see sehen
she sie
shop assistant Verkäufer/in
short kurz
shoulder Schulter
show zeigen
sight Sehenswürdigkeit
sing singen
sister Schwester

sit sitzen
skeleton Skelett
ski Ski, Ski fahren
small klein
snake Schlange
snap schnipsen
snowdrop Schneeglöckchen
snowy verschneit
speak sprechen
spider Spinne
sports Sportarten
spring Frühling
stamp aufstampfen
stone Stein
straight ahead geradeaus
street Straße
stretch dehnen, strecken
strong stark
subject Fach, Schulfach
summer Sommer
Sunday Sonntag
sunny sonnig
sweets Süßigkeiten
swim schwimmen

T

table Tisch
table tennis Tischtennis
tail Schwanz
talk reden
taxi Taxi
taxi driver Taxifahrer/in
tea Tee
teacher Lehrer/in
temperature Temperatur
tennis Tennis
text message, SMS SMS
there dort
they sie
this diese/r/s
throw werfen
Thursday Donnerstag
ticket Fahrkarte
tiger Tiger
time Zeit
timetable Stundenplan
to nach, zu
today heute
toe Zeh
toilet Toilette
tomato/es Tomate, Tomaten
tooth, teeth Zahn, Zähne
touch anfassen, berühren
train Zug
treason Verrat
tree Baum
Tuesday Dienstag
tummy Bauch
turn abbiegen
turn around umdrehen

U

uncle Onkel
under unter
underground U-Bahn
understand verstehen
upstairs oben
USA USA (= Vereinigte Staaten von Amerika)
useful nützlich

V

Vampire Vampir

W

walk gehen
want wollen
watching TV fernsehen
water Wasser
we wir
weather Wetter
weather report Wetterbericht
Wednesday Mittwoch
weekend Wochenende
welcome willkommen
whale Wal
what was
wheel Rad
when wann
where wo
who wer
why warum
wiggle hin und her bewegen, zappeln
wild wild
windy windig
winter Winter
wish wünschen
witch Hexe

Word list

Deutsch – Englisch

A

abbiegen turn
Abend evening
Abendessen dinner
Affe monkey
alt old
anfassen touch
anschauen look at
antworten answer
auf on
auf und ab bewegen flap
aufstampfen stamp
auf ... zeigen point to
Auge eye
aus from
ausmalen colour (in)
ausschneiden cut out
aussetzen miss a turn
Auto car

B

Ballett ballet
Ballett machen do ballet
Basketball basketball
Bauch belly, tummy
Baum tree
bei at
Bein leg
Beruf job
berühmt famous
berühren touch
beugen bend
(sich) bewegen move
Bild picture
bitte please
Blatt, Blätter leaf, leaves
Boot boat
Brot bread
Bruder brother
Buch book
Bus bus
Busch bush
Busfahrer/in bus driver
Butter butter

C

Cent cent
Computer (Schulfach) Computers (I.C.T.)

D

Datum date
dehnen stretch
Deutsch (Schulfach), deutsch German
Deutschland Germany
Dienstag Tuesday
diese/r/s this
Dinosaurier dinosaur
Dollar ($) dollar
Donnerstag Thursday
dort there
Drachen kite
Dschungel jungle
Du meine Güte! Goodness gracious!

E

Ei egg
Elefant elephant
E-Mail email
E-Mail-Freund/in e-pal
England England
Englisch (Schulfach), englisch English
er he
erinnern remember
es it
essen eat
Essen food
Euro (€) euro

F

Fach, Schulfach subject
Fahrer driver
Fahrkarte ticket
Farbe colour
Ferien holidays
fernsehen watching TV
Feuerwerk fireworks
Flagge flag
fliegen fly
Flugzeug plane
Fluss river
Foto photo
fragen ask
Freitag Friday
Freunde treffen meeting friends
Friseur/in hairdresser
Frühling spring
Frühstück breakfast
Fuß, Füße foot, feet
Fußball football
füttern feed

G

geben give
gefährlich dangerous

gehen go, walk
Geist ghost
geradeaus straight ahead
geschehen happen
Geschenk present
Getränk drink
Giraffe giraffe
Glockenturm clock tower
glücklich happy
Grad degree(s)
groß big
Großbritannien Great Britain
Großmutter grandmother
Großstadt city
Großvater grandfather

H

haben have (got)
halb (Uhrzeit) half past
hallo hello
Halloween Halloween
hassen hate
Haus house
Hausmeister caretaker
heiß hot
helfen help
Herbst autumn
heute today
Hexe witch
hier here
hin und her bewegen, zappeln wiggle
Hilfe help
hilfreich helpful
Hobby hobby
hoffen hope
hopsen hop
Huhn chicken

I

Idee idea
ihr, ihre her, its
in in
ist is

J

Jahreszeit season
Job job
Judo judo
Judo betreiben do judo

K

Kalender calendar
Kamel camel
Käse cheese
kaufen buy
kennen know
Klasse class
Klassenraum classroom
klatschen clap
kleben glue
Klebstift glue stick
Kleid dress
klein little, small
Klub, AG, Verein club
Knie knee
kommen come
König king
Königin queen
können can
Kopf head
Kopfsalat lettuce
krank ill
Krokodil crocodile
Kunst (Schulfach) Art
Kürbis pumpkin
kurz short

L

Lagerfeuer bonfire
lang long
laufen run
laut loud, loudly
leben, wohnen live
legen put
Lehrer/in teacher
leise quiet
lesen read
Liebe/r ... Dear ...
Liebe Grüße ... Love, ...
lieben love
Lieblings- favourite
lila purple
Linie line
links left
Los! Let's go!
Löwe lion

M

machen do, make
Mathe (Schulfach) Maths
Mechaniker/in mechanic
Meer sea
mein/e my

Word list

Deutsch–Englisch

Mittagessen lunch
Mittwoch Wednesday
Montag Monday
Morgen morning
Motorrad motorbike
Museum museum
Musik (Schulfach) Music
Musik hören listening to music
müssen have to
Mutter mother

N

nach, zu to
Nachmittag afternoon
Name name
Nase nose
natürlich of course
neben next to
neblig foggy
nett nice
nicht not
Nilpferd hippo
noch einmal again
Noten, Notizen notes
Nummer number
nützlich useful

O

oben upstairs
offen open
Ohr ear
Oma grandma
Onkel uncle
Opa grandpa
Osterglocke daffodil

P

Papagei parrot
Papier paper
Passwort password
Pferd horse
Polizeiwache police station
Polizist/in police officer
Pommes frites chips
Postkarte postcard

R

Rad wheel
rechts right
reden talk
regnerisch rainy
Reihe line
Reim rhyme
reiten ride a horse
Rose rose
Rücken back

S

Sachunterricht (Schulfach) Science
sagen say
Salat (zubereitet) salad
Samstag Saturday
Savanne savannah
Schießpulver gunpowder
Schinken ham
Schlange snake
schlecht bad
Schneeglöckchen snowdrop
schnipsen snap
Schokolade chocolate
Schüler/in pupil
Schulfach (school) subject
Schulstunde lesson
Schulter shoulder
Schwanz tail
Schwester sister
schwimmen swim
sehen look, see
Sehenswürdigkeit sight
sein be
sein/e his
sein/e, ihr/e its
sie she, they
singen sing
sitzen sit
Skelett skeleton
Ski, Ski fahren ski
SMS SMS, text message
Sommer summer
sonnig sunny
Sonntag Sunday
spät late
Spiel game
spielen play
Spinne spider
Spitzname nickname
Sport (Schulfach) P.E. (= Physical Education)
Sportarten sports
sprechen speak
springen jump
stark strong
Stein stone

stellen put
Straße street
strecken stretch
Stuhl chair
Stundenplan timetable
Süßigkeiten sweets

T

Tafel blackboard
Tag day
Tante aunt
tanzen dance
Taxi taxi
Taxifahrer/in taxi driver
Tee tea
Temperatur temperature
Tennis tennis
Teppich carpet
Theaterspiel play
Tier animal
Tiger tiger
Tisch table
Tischtennis table tennis
Toilette toilet
Tomate/n tomato/es
Traum dream
traurig sad
trinken drink
Tür door

U

U-Bahn underground
über about
Uhr clock, … o'clock
um at
umdrehen turn around
unten downstairs
unter under
USA (Vereinigte Staaten von Amerika) USA

V

Vampir vampire
Vater father
verängstigt scared
verärgert angry
vergessen forget
Verkäufer/in shop assistant
Verrat treason
verschneit snowy
Verschwörung plot
verstehen understand
viel much
viel/e many
Viel Glück! Good luck!
viertel vor/nach (Uhrzeit) quarter to/past
von from
vor in front of
vorwärts forward

W

Wal whale
wann when
warm hot
warum why
was what
Wasser water
Weihnachten Christmas
Weihnachtsmann Father Christmas, Santa Claus (USA)
weil because
wer who
werfen throw
Wetter weather
Wetterbericht weather report
wie how
wie viel how much
wie viele how many
wild wild
willkommen welcome
windig windy
Winter winter
wir we
wissen know
wo where
Wochenende weekend
wohnen live
wolkig cloudy
wollen want
wünschen wish

Z

Zahn, Zähne tooth, teeth
Zeh toe
zeichnen draw
zeigen show
Zeit time
zu to
Zug train
zu Hause (at) home

Sunshine

Lehrwerk für den früh beginnenden Englischunterricht

Pupil's Book 4

Englisch ab Klasse 1

Erarbeitet von
Tanja Beattie, Ebersberg; Stefanie Keller, Konstanz; Nadine Kerler, Ulm; Daniela Röbers, Erkelenz; Caroline Schröder, München; Maria Skejic, Frankfurt am Main; Gertrud Steinhausen, Ratingen

Auf der Grundlage der Ausgabe von
Birgit Hollbrügge, Bielefeld; Ulrike Kraaz, Werther

Beratende Mitwirkung
Uwe Becker, Mannheim; Margit Butscher-Wich, Bad Abbach; Michael Duscha, Braunschweig; Renate Hafner, Blaustein; Siân Williams-Hahn, Schorndorf (englischsprachige Texte)

Verlagsredaktion
Daniela Aue

Illustration
Christian Bartz, Berlin; Beehive Illustration, Cirencester, England: Neil Chapman, Mike Phillips; Raimo Bergt, Berlin; Volker Fredrich, Hamburg; Mary Hall, Bath, England; Jan Lewis, Pangbourne, England

Gesamtgestaltung
Corinna Babylon, Berlin

Technische Umsetzung
Corngreen GmbH, Leipzig

www.cornelsen.de

1. Auflage, 2. Druck 2021

Alle Drucke dieser Auflage sind inhaltlich unverändert und können im Unterricht nebeneinander verwendet werden.

Druck: Athesiadruck GmbH

ISBN 978-3-06-083981-0 (Schülerbuch)
ISBN 978-3-06-084043-4 (E-Book)

PEFC
PEFC/10-31-100

PEFC zertifiziert
Dieses Produkt stammt aus nachhaltig bewirtschafteten Wäldern und kontrollierten Quellen.

www.pefc.de